The Tiger Has a Toothache

Helping Animals at the Zoo

By Patricia Lauber

Illustrated by
Mary Morgan

NATIONAL GEOGRAPHIC SOCIETY

Washington, D.C.

The author wishes to thank Paul Calle, DVM, Dipl. ACZM,
Senior Veterinarian, Department of Clinical Studies, Wildlife Conservation
Society, for his generous help and Lucy H. Spelman, DVM, Dipl. ACZM,
Associate Veterinarian, National Zoological Park, for her helpful comments.
The illustrator would like to thank William Kirk Suedmeyer, DVM, Senior Staff Veterinarian
at the Kansas City Zoological Gardens, for his kind assistance.

The decorative element on the title page is inspired by Rainey Gate,
an entrance to the Bronx Zoo, headquarters for the
Wildlife Conservation Society.
The paintings in this book are rendered in watercolor and pen and ink on Strathmore 100 percent rag paper.

Library of Congress Cataloging-in-Publication Data
Lauber, Patricia
The Tiger Has a Toothache : Helping Animals at the Zoo / Patricia Lauber ; illustrated by Mary Morgan
p. cm.
Summary: Examines the work of zoo veterinarians focusing on such cases as a tiger with a toothache,
a gorilla with a cold, and a tortoise with a broken bone.
ISBN 0-7922-3441-3 (hardcover) 0-7922-8234-5 (paperback)
1. Zoo animals—Diseases—Juvenile literature. 2. Veterinary medicine—Juvenile literature. [1. Zoo animals—
Diseases. 2. Zoo veterinarians. 3. Veterinary medicine.] I. Morgan-Vanroyen, Mary, 1957- II. Title
SF996.L38 1999

636.089'6—dc21   97-38635

One of the world's largest nonprofit scientific and educational organizations, the National Geographic Society
was founded in 1888 "for the increase and diffusion of geographic knowledge." Fulfilling this mission, the Society
educates and inspires millions every day through its magazines, books, television programs, videos, maps and atlases,
research grants, the National Geographic Bee, teacher workshops, and innovative classroom materials. The Society is
supported through membership dues, charitable gifts, and income from the sale of its educational products. This support
is vital to National Geographic's mission to increase global understanding and promote conservation of our planet
through exploration, research, and education.

For more information, please call
1-800-NGS-LINE (647-5463) or write to the following address:

National Geographic Society
1145 17th Street N.W.
Washington, D.C. 20036-4688
U.S.A.

Visit the Society's Web site: www.nationalgeographic.com

*How Vets and Keepers
Helped the*

The Tiger

It's morning at the zoo. A keeper has been watching the tigers. Her job is to take care of them. She is with them every day, and she knows them the way owners know their pets. This morning she is worried about the tiger called George.

George is unhappy. He has lost his pep. He is cross. And he hasn't eaten. Upset stomach? the keeper wonders. Or perhaps George has sore gums or a bad tooth. The keeper thinks George needs a doctor.

This big zoo has several animal doctors, or veterinarians. They are called vets for short. The vets take care of animals that are sick or injured. They also help animals to stay well by giving them shots. The shots keep the animals from catching certain diseases.

It would be dangerous to walk up to an animal like a tiger and give it a shot with a big needle. So the vets use darts, which carry medicine. The darts are shot from a blowpipe or an air gun.

The animals don't like the darts. Many are smart enough to remember who shot them. When George sees the vet, he opens his mouth and snarls.

This is good. Now the vet can see into George's mouth. What he sees is a broken tooth. No wonder George is cross and won't eat. The tiger has a toothache. It hurts!

The tooth needs to be fixed. No one can touch it while the tiger is awake. The vet shoots him with a dart. It carries a drug that sends George into a deep sleep. This kind of drug is called an anesthetic.

A couple of people roll the sleeping tiger onto a canvas. The canvas is lifted onto a stretcher. The stretcher goes into an animal ambulance that carries George to the zoo's hospital. It is much like a hospital for people.

The vet looks at the tooth. George must have closed his powerful jaws on something hard, like a stone. When he did, the tip of the tooth broke off. The vet can see the soft matter inside. It holds nerves. When anything touches the nerves, the tiger's jaw hurts.

Sometimes the zoo asks a dentist to work on an animal's tooth. But the vet decides he can do this job himself. He cleans out the tooth, fills it, and seals the top. He also cleans George's teeth.

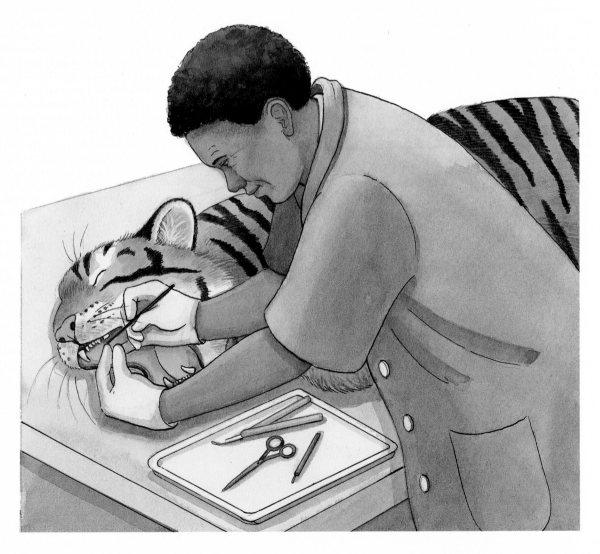

This is a good chance to check the tiger over—to weigh him, take his temperature, listen to his heart and lungs. The exam shows that George is healthy.

Now the tiger is taken home. Still sleeping, he is put down in a quiet area with dim light. When George wakes, he will be in his own place. A few hours later he will feel like himself—hungry, peppy, and happy.

The Frog

Freddy has swallowed a stone.

Freddy is a rare kind of frog. Because he is red, he is called a tomato frog.

Like all frogs, Freddy sometimes makes a mistake. He was watching a cricket hop within reach. As the cricket hopped onto a small stone, Freddy's long, sticky tongue flicked out. It picked up the cricket and the stone. Freddy swallowed them both. Now he doesn't feel well. He is quiet, not lively. His keeper sees that Freddy needs a doctor. The frog is picked up and taken to the hospital.

A vet thinks Freddy has swallowed something he shouldn't have. But she needs to make sure. To see inside the frog, she takes an x-ray picture. It shows a stone in his stomach.

Now the vet mixes an anesthetic with water and puts Freddy
in the water. The drug passes through his skin into his body.
It makes Freddy go to sleep.

To get the stone, the vet uses a thin tube that bends.
She slides it down the frog's throat. The tube carries light so
that the vet can see inside the stomach. It also holds a pair of tiny
grippers. They are folded up inside the tube. They open when they
are pushed out. The vet uses them to grip the stone. She gently
pulls the tube out of the frog. The stone comes out too.

Soon Freddy will be back at his pond, as good as new.

The Gorilla

Herb the gorilla has a cold. He coughs. He sneezes. His nose runs. Like a person with a bad cold, he feels terrible. He also looks terrible. Gorillas don't use handkerchiefs.

Colds are caused by germs. One gorilla can catch another's cold. Gorillas can also catch colds from people. That is why vets and keepers wear masks near gorillas. They do not want to give the animals germs by coughing or sneezing on them. Visitors to the zoo may not be as careful.

Signs say, Please Do Not Feed the Animals. Some people do anyway. They may eat part of an apple, for example, and throw the rest to a gorilla. A person with a cold is also throwing cold germs to the gorilla. That is how Herb caught a cold.

If a gorilla has a cold, he is watched carefully. He may take the same cough medicine that people take. It is mixed with fruit juice or something else he likes. If he gets worse, he is given other medicines. But usually the cold goes away after a few days or a week. Like a person who is over a cold, the gorilla feels fine again.

The Snake

The snake can't lay her eggs. The keeper sees her try, but no eggs appear. Not long ago the snake was sick. She is getting better, but she is not well enough to lay eggs. She needs help.

The snake is a big one—a Burmese python called Susie. It takes four keepers to get her to the hospital.

The vet wants to make sure that Susie is ready to lay her eggs. He uses a machine that sends sound waves into her body. When the sound waves echo back, they form a picture on a screen. The picture shows that the eggs are ready to be laid. There are dozens and dozens of them.

Susie is given an anesthetic to make her sleep. The vet operates on her, removes the eggs, and sews up the slit he made. Susie can go home now.

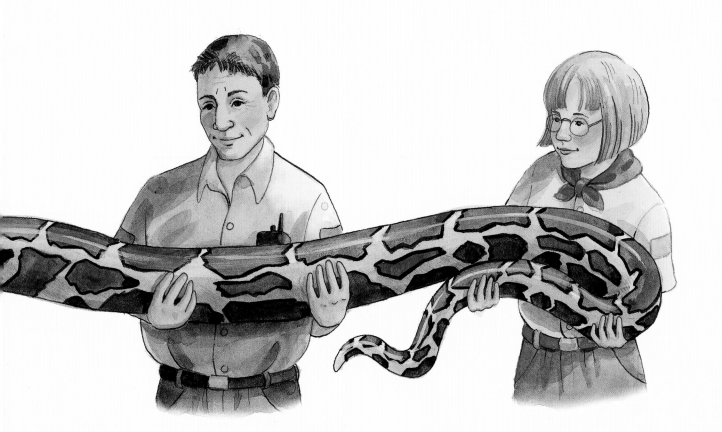

Most snake eggs hatch by themselves. The mother snake lays them and goes away. But Burmese pythons stay with their eggs. The mother gathers them and coils around them. She keeps twitching. In this way, she warms her body, which warms the eggs. She warms them for about two months.

Susie's eggs need warming, but the zoo has no room for dozens of pythons. The vet chooses a few eggs and places them in a warm box called an incubator. They will hatch there.

Once the young wiggle out of their leathery eggshells, they are ready to hunt. They can find their own food and take care of themselves. They will be turned loose where Susie lives at the zoo.

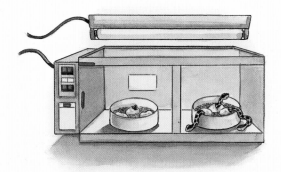

The Parrot

Polly the parrot has lost her voice. Yesterday she was happily squawking and calling out, "Hello, Jo! Leave the bird food here." Today she is not talking, and sometimes she coughs. She opens her beak, but no sound comes out. The keeper misses Polly's voice.

A vet sends Polly to the hospital. She is wrapped in a towel so that she can't struggle and hurt herself.

17

Parrots have strong beaks. The vet has to pry Polly's open. He places a big metal ring in the beak to keep it open. Now he discovers what is wrong. Polly has a seed stuck in her windpipe. Probably she was excited and eating too fast. She breathed at the wrong time and drew a seed into her windpipe.

Polly is given an anesthetic to send her to sleep. To get the seed, the vet uses the same sort of thin tube that was used to take the stone out of Freddy's stomach. He slides it into Polly's windpipe and gently removes the seed.

Soon Polly is squawking and talking again. She is still telling Jo where to put the bird food. But now she has something new to say: "Feeling better Polly? That's good, that's good."

The Elephant

Ellie the elephant is having her nails done.

In the wild, elephants walk far and wear down their nails. In a zoo, nails must be trimmed.

Elephants are animals that can be trained. Ellie's keeper has trained her to pick up one foot and rest it on a stool. He uses a large file to trim each nail. Ellie is an African elephant, with five nails on each front foot and three on each hind foot. The keeper does each foot in turn. Because Ellie did as she was asked, the keeper rewards her with peanuts.

One time, while walking with a friend, Ellie got a little pebble stuck between a nail and the skin. The pebble gave her a sore toe. Ellie began to limp. When the keeper saw the limp, he knew something was wrong and sent for a doctor.

A vet came to treat Ellie, but he did not have to give her an anesthetic. Ellie had been trained to let a vet help her. He took the pebble out and gave the keeper medicine for the toe. He said Ellie was to soak her foot several times a day in a bucket of warm water and Epsom salts.

The keeper gave Ellie two apples and a banana for being a good elephant.

The Bat

The baby bat needs help. His mother wasn't taking care of him. And so he is being raised in the zoo's nursery. The keepers there call him Benny.

Most mother animals take good care of their young. But mothers may be sick and not able to care for their babies. Some young mothers seem not to know how. And some mothers, like Benny's, just don't—no one knows why. All babies that need help are brought to the nursery.

Benny and his mother are fruit bats of a rare kind. Fruit bats live in warm parts of the world where there is fruit to eat all year round. By day, they roost and sleep in trees. Roosting, they hang head down from branches, holding on with the claws of their hind feet. They feed at night.

When a mother flies out to feed, the baby goes too. It clings to her underside with its teeth and claws. When they return, the mother hangs by her hind claws. She folds her wings around the baby, which nurses and sleeps upside down.

At the nursery, Benny is kept warm in an incubator. He sucks milk from a nipple. He hangs head down from what looks like a soft, stuffed sock. A dark cloth is draped over Benny, to take the place of the mother's wings.

When he is older, the young bat will be given fruit to eat. He will be taken to see other bats hanging from trees and flying out to feed. That way he will learn what bats do. When Benny is big enough, he will join the others.

The Penguin

One rockhopper penguin feels sick. The other rockhoppers are busy doing what rockhoppers do—hopping. They are hopping from rock to rock, hopping into their pool and out again. The one called Cassidy stands apart. He is not hopping. He is not swimming. The keeper sees he is an unhappy penguin. She wonders if Cassidy has swallowed a coin.

Some zoo visitors treat the pools and ponds as wishing wells. They throw coins into the water. This is bad for animals that eat fish. They see a shiny thing shimmering down through the water, think it is food, and swallow it. Some coins are made mostly of a metal called zinc. They are the worst of all. They poison the animals.

There is no time to waste if Cassidy has swallowed zinc. He is whisked off to the hospital.

A mask is put on the penguin's head. He breathes in a gas that is an anesthetic. X-ray pictures show a coin in his stomach. A blood test shows zinc in his blood.

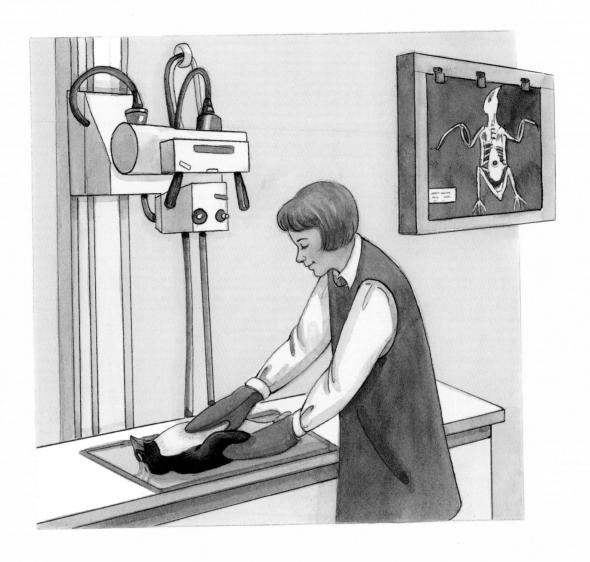

A vet takes the coin out of Cassidy's stomach, using the tube with grippers. But the zinc in his blood means that Cassidy is a sick penguin. He will have to stay in the hospital and take medicine until he is better. Then he can go back to his pool.

The Giraffe

The giraffe called Mary Lou ought to be having a baby. But so far the baby hasn't been born.

Animals like to have their babies when the zoo is quiet and no one is around. Every morning the keeper goes to the stall where Mary Lou lives, hoping to see a baby giraffe. The keeper and the vets are starting to worry.

Perhaps a bent leg or a bent neck is keeping the baby from being born. If so, they will have to put Mary Lou in a chute that holds her still. They will give her a shot to make her calm and sleepy. Then a vet can reach inside her and help the baby. He can straighten the leg or neck so that the baby slides out.

The vet doesn't want to do this. Mary Lou will be half asleep when her baby is born. She may not know the baby belongs to her and may refuse to nurse it. Then the baby will have to be cared for by keepers and fed by hand. It's better for a baby to be with its mother. The vet decides to wait two more days.

On the second morning, the keeper goes to Mary Lou's stall, and there it is! Six feet tall, a healthy young giraffe is standing shyly beside its mother. All is well.

The Tortoise

The tortoise called Rosa has hurt herself. Yesterday she was walking around on all four legs. Today she is trying to walk on three. She doesn't want to eat. And she is clearly in pain. Her keeper thinks Rosa must have fallen.

A vet says Rosa needs x-rays taken. The x-ray pictures will show if any leg bones are broken.

Rosa is a big tortoise. Some of her relatives are 4 feet long and weigh 500 pounds. If Rosa were that big, the vet would bring an x-ray machine to the tortoise. But Rosa is smaller. She weighs only 150 pounds. She is small enough to be picked up and taken to the hospital.

The x-ray pictures show a broken bone. Rosa is given an anesthetic. The vet cuts into her leg over the broken bone. He uses a metal pin to hold the pieces together. Then he sews up the leg.

A tortoise can't use crutches. How will Rosa get around while the bone is mending?

The vet decides to give her wheels. He fits a skateboard to the corner of her shell. Now she can keep her broken leg inside her shell and use her three good legs to push herself around.

Be a Good Visitor

People at zoos work hard to keep their animals healthy and happy. If an animal is sick or injured, keepers and vets do their best to help. For them this work is much more than a job. They care about the animals. They feel responsible for them. They feel the way good pet owners do.

You, too, can help the animals by being a good zoo visitor.

- A good visitor never feeds the animals unless the zoo says it's all right.

- A good visitor never throws coins into ponds or pools.

- A good visitor never teases the animals.

- A good zoo visitor looks, listens, reads, learns— and has a wonderful time watching the animals.